Series / Number 04-025

Community Status and Conflict
in Suburban School Politics

WILLIAM L. BOYD
University of Rochester

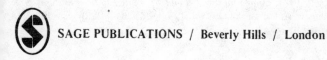

SAGE PUBLICATIONS / Beverly Hills / London

For information address:

SAGE PUBLICATIONS, INC.
275 South Beverly Drive
Beverly Hills, California 90212

SAGE PUBLICATIONS LTD
St George's House / 44 Hatton Garden
London EC1N 8ER

International Standard Book Number 0-8039-0537-8

Library of Congress Catalog Card No. 74-27564

FIRST PRINTING

When citing a professional paper, please use the proper form. Remember to cite the
correct Sage Professional Paper series title and include the paper number. One of the
two following formats can be adapted (depending on the style manual used):

(1) NAGEL, S. S. (1973) "Comparing Elected and Appointed Judicial Systems."
Sage Professional Papers in American Politics, 1, 04-001. Beverly Hills, and London:
Sage Pubns.

OR

(2) Nagel, Stuart S. 1973. *Comparing Elected and Appointed Judicial Systems.* Sage
Professional Papers in American Politics, vol. 1, series no. 04-001. Beverly Hills and
London: Sage Publications.

CONTENTS

Community Status and Conflict
in Suburban School Politics

WILLIAM L. BOYD
University of Rochester

INTRODUCTION

Although public school districts represent America's most numerous
governmental units—and expend the largest proportion of local public
revenues—a concerted and systematic exploration of American school
politics has only begun in recent years.[1] Because of the exceptional
social, political, and educational problems confronted by our large city
school systems, they have naturally commanded most of the attention of
researchers interested in school politics.[2] However, with the growing
concentration of Americans in suburban areas, systematic knowledge
about the nature of suburban school politics becomes increasingly important.[3] While much of the research on suburban school politics to date
consists of atheoretical single case studies, whose richness in data tends to
be offset by its limited generalizability, an important exception to this
rule is found in a pair of related comparative studies by David Minar
(1966a; 1966b), which raise a number of intriguing questions concerning
the effects of community socioeconomic status upon conflict in educational policymaking.[4] These questions prompted the research reported
here, which used Minar's pioneering work as a point of departure for a
comparative case study investigating the factors affecting the incidence
and intensity of conflict in high and low status suburban school districts.

AUTHOR'S NOTE: *This is a substantially revised and expanded version of a paper
presented at the annual meeting of the American Educational Research Association,
April 5, 1972, Chicago. A revised, abridged version of this paper is included in* The
Polity of the School: New Research in Educational Politics, *edited by Frederick Wirt
(Lexington, Mass.: Heath, 1975). I wish to acknowledge with gratitude the helpful
comments of Paul Peterson and Charles Bidwell on earlier versions of this paper.*

Of course, however interesting conflict and its causes may be in themselves, it is clear that not all conflict in school politics has significant immediate or long-term consequences. However, studies of American public school politics suggest that *high* levels of public conflict in educational policymaking have at least three important consequences. First, there is evidence that as the level of conflict in school district policymaking increases, the autonomy and discretion of school administrators are reduced as a result of increased school board and citizen involvement in, and scrutiny of, the policymaking process (Minar 1966a; 1966b).[5] Second, there is evidence that high levels of conflict tend to have a debilitating effect on school officials (Campbell, 1968; Minar, 1966b). As Minar notes (1967: 37), because of the widespread belief that the governance of education should be nonpolitical and nonpartisan,

> the [school] authority system usually is not accustomed to being opposed and therefore lacks resilience. Conflict is likely to be a disorganizing shock. Whereas, in most democratic government, structured conflict is recognized as the way the game is played, in school government it often seems to be regarded as a rude and foreign intrusion.

Finally, research shows that conflict which continues and increases over time is likely to lead, ultimately, to the defeat of school board members seeking reelection, followed by the replacement of the school superintendent and the adoption of new educational policies (Iannaccone, 1967). Since most recent studies have concluded that educators generally dominate most aspects of public school policymaking (Kirst, 1970: v-16; Peterson, 1974), the reduction of the autonomy and influence of school administrators is in itself a significant development, making possible—but by no means ensuring—a more democratic policymaking process.[6]

If the consequences of high levels of conflict in school politics are significant, then knowledge about the factors causing and influencing the course of such conflict is important.[7] Although the literature on school politics and community conflict suggests a variety of factors affecting conflict, Minar (1966a, 1966b) has presented data indicating that the likelihood of high levels of conflict and reduced discretion for school administrators varies *primarily* with the socioeconomic status of communities. In a study of 48 Chicago suburban elementary school districts, Minar (1966a) found that the 24 higher status districts had substantially lower levels of electoral *conflict* (as measured by votes cast for losing candidates) and electoral *participation* in school board elections than did the 24 lower status districts. In addition, he found that the school superintendents in lower status districts were much more likely to have minor administrative decisions and policies questioned by their school boards than were their counterparts in the higher status districts.

From these and other related data, Minar concluded that the variable which could best account for his findings was the differential possession by higher and lower status school districts of resources of conflict management skills in their respective populaces. By conflict management resources, Minar meant the aggregate organizational and management skills and associated attitudes derived from the level of education and the kinds of occupations of a given populace. Minar hypothesized (1966a: 827) that the greater possession of management resources (including skills in such areas as "communication, negotiation, persuasion, division of labor, and delegation of function") by higher than by lower status districts promoted deference to expertise (that is, deference to professional administrators) in the former districts and tended to lead to a controlling and channelling of the educational decision-making process (especially by means of the use of nominating caucuses for the selection of school board candidates) in such a way as to minimize conflict. Conversely, Minar argued that the paucity of management resources in lower status districts is likely to reduce deference to expertise, increase school board and citizen interference in essentially administrative, as opposed to policy, matters, and reduce the community's ability to contain and control conflict.

In a followup comparative case study of four of the original 48 districts, Minar (1966b) explored the validity of his hypothesis and concluded that it was essentially correct. However, because Minar chose to select for in-depth study two high status/low conflict districts and two low status/high conflict districts, there was no common effect between the pairs of districts. By not including what according to the *conflict management resources* hypothesis would be the *deviant* cases (that is, high status/high conflict districts and low status/low conflict districts), the design of the study tended to make the rejection of the hypothesis unlikely. This is a troublesome point, for although the logic of the hypothesis is quite appealing in some respects, it seems to provide almost too simple an explanation for such complex phenomena. Indeed, it places a heavy burden upon the instrumental and rational aspects of political behavior—and upon the value placed on efficiency and objectivity in community decision-making—with little regard for the subjective aspects of political behavior and decision-making. But, when controversial issues arise, emotional and irrational responses tend to be triggered which frequently lead to conflict. It seems unlikely that abundant management resources by themselves could prevent or suppress these responses to the extent that conflict would nearly always be avoided or held to a low level. Also, it seems implausible that plentiful management resources could consistently prevent controversial issues from arising in the first place.[8]

In fact, political and sociological theory suggest a number of plausible rival explanations, some of which Minar acknowledged and considered, within the limitations of his data and research design. For example, it could be argued that:

(1) lower status communities are more likely to be conflictual because, unlike their more affluent higher status counterparts, their cost of governmental services is a continuing and burdensome issue;

(2) the higher levels of education of higher status populaces lead them to value education and other governmental services more and hence be more willing—as well as more able—to spend for these services than lower status populaces (see James et al., 1963);

(3) higher status populaces tend to be "civic-minded" and supportive of government (see Banfield and Wilson, 1963) while

(4) lower status populaces are inclined to be "alienated" and hostile toward government (see Levin, 1960; Horton and Thompson, 1962); and

(5) lower status communities may be less well integrated due to their low levels of citizen participation and the concomitant weakness of their organizational networks; hence, they may be more susceptible to conflict (Coleman, 1957; Kornhauser, 1959).

Although Minar recognized that explanations such as these may account for some part of the variance in conflict he found, he vigorously maintained that the single most potent variable is the differential possession of conflict management resources by higher and lower status districts.

Of course Minar did not claim that his hypothesis could account for all phenomena of school politics, but instead he argued for its general applicability. As he noted, "such questions as what happens to low conflict communities in the event of a deep ideological schism or what happens to a high conflict community in the presence of extraordinarily skilled technical leadership remain substantially untouched" (1966a: 833).[9] Thus, the present study sought to test Minar's hypothesis through a design which included "deviant" as well as "nondeviant" cases. By this approach, it was possible to investigate both the factors operating in the absence of plentiful management resources to minimize conflict in low status/low conflict districts and the factors appearing to account for the ineffectiveness of the abundant management resources in high status/high conflict districts. Equally important, the study was designed to provide a more adequate test of possible alternative explanations for Minar's findings, such as those enumerated above.

Utilizing a sample of four lower status and four higher status Chicago suburban elementary school districts for comparative analysis, it became clear that the political culture or "ethos" of the school districts studied—which varied with community status—was at least as important as their relative possession of conflict management resources; indeed, it was more significant in "explaining" much of the variance in conflict and other aspects of political behavior. This was an unexpected finding because the arena associated with the "political ethos" theory (see Banfield and Wilson, 1963) is the rough and tumble world of big city politics with which suburban school districts are generally thought to have little in common.

CONCEPTUAL FRAMEWORK AND RESEARCH DESIGN

Theorists have emphasized the significant consequences of community status for both the *normative* structure (that is, the system of norms, values, and roles) and the *social* structure (that is, the system of social relationships) of communities.[10] Since there is a reciprocal relationship between the normative structure and the social structure (see Scott, 1970: 102-108), and since both may affect community conflict propensity—and, indeed, in combination may have multiplicative rather than simply additive effects—it is clearly important to attempt to take account of significant factors in both dimensions when endeavoring to explain differences among communities in their experiences with conflict.[11] Our approach took its point of departure from the fact that much of the research on community conflict, including Minar's work, suggests that the way in which community status conditions citizen participation—through shaping both the normative and social structures of the community—is a key factor influencing the incidence and intensity of conflict. Thus, in conceptualizing our research problem, we expected that community status would influence both the rate and type of citizen participation in educational policymaking and the behavior of the school board and superintendent, that citizen participation and school board and superintendent behavior would influence one another, and that they would both influence and be influenced by the incidence and intensity of conflict in educational policymaking. Furthermore, we expected that aspects of the community social structure and power structure[12] might promote or inhibit both citizen participation and conflict, and would thus have to be taken into account in appraising the effect of community status upon participation and conflict. Finally, we assumed that the fundamental aspects of citizen participation, school board and superintendent behavior, and conflict in educational policymaking would be revealed by focusing upon what Easton (1965) conceptualizes as the essential inputs of a political system, *demands* and *support*——that is, the presentation to and processing of demands by the authorities and the pursuit and provision of support for the authorities.[13]

In order to study the effects of community socioeconomic status upon citizen participation and the incidence and intensity of conflict in educational policymaking, a sample of eight districts was selected from the 118 Cook County suburban elementary school districts to provide pairs of districts to fill the cells of a fourfold typology (see Figure 1) of community status (as measured by 1960 median family income) and known conflict (as indicated by performance in tax and bond referenda from 1963 through 1968).[14] Table 1 presents data reflecting differences in status characteristics and the availability of conflict management resources among the eight districts. It was assumed that districts which had defeated two or more referenda from 1963 through 1968 would tend to be districts high in conflict in general, while districts which had held referenda during this period without defeat would tend to be districts low on overall conflict. As it developed, this assumption was born out by the case study data collected.

Following Minar (1966a), conflict in educational decision-making was defined as the "public confrontation of competing demands" and included all publicly manifested demands pertaining to school affairs, for example, in public meetings, in the newspapers, by picketing, and in elections. It was necessary, at the outset, however, to distinguish between two principal types of conflict. On the one hand there is *voting* or *electoral* conflict, which can

		Conflict in Referenda	
		Low	High
Community Status	High	Northview (1) Oakton (4) TYPE I	Greenwood (2) Camden (3) TYPE II
	Low	Smithville (6) Trenton (8) TYPE III	Alton (5) Weston (7) TYPE IV

Figure 1: DISTRICTS SELECTED CLASSIFIED ACCORDING TO COMMUNITY STATUS (RANKED BY NUMBER) AND CONFLICT IN REFERENDA

TABLE 1

Selected Data Reflecting Community Status and the Availability of Conflict Management Resources

District Type	Northview I	Greenwood II	Camden II	Oakton I	Alton IV	Smithville III	Weston IV	Trenton III
Education: Proportion of the total population 25 and over who are:								
Elementary Educated:	11	20	16	19	35	37	34	49
High School Educated:	28	34	45	53	53	49	58	40
College Educated:	61	46	38	28	11	14	8	6
Income: Proportion of all families with 1959 annual income levels:								
Less than $7,000	15	22	19	23	41	44	43	51
$7,000 to $9,999	8	16	24	35	34	31	37	29
$10,000 or more	77	62	57	41	24	26	20	20
Employment: Proportion of total employed persons in the following job classifications:								
Craftsman, Operatives or Laborers:	6	15	18	32	48	42	59	59
Professional-Managerial:	49	40	43	28	14	18	10	9

aSource: U.S. Census, 1960, Tables P-1 and P-3.

be readily operationalized as the proportion of votes cast for losing candidates in school board elections and the proportion of dissenting votes cast in referenda. Conflict occuring *between elections,* on the other hand, is more difficult to operationalize. The measure chosen was the extent to which demands arise in the community, from students or employees of the school system, or from certain school board members, which the majority on the board or the superintendent perceive as in competition with, or opposition to, their program, policies, or desires, or in competition with other demands being presented to the board or superintendent.

The business of making a comparative case analysis involving variables such as conflict between elections, for which the data are wholly or mainly qualitative, inescapably presents some serious methodological problems. The method adopted in this study was modeled after procedures employed by Crain and his associates (1969) in an analogous research problem—their comparative analysis of the school desegregation issue in eight northern cities. They elected to develop rank orderings of the cities on variables, such as total civil rights activity, for which they could not produce "hard" numerical data to demonstrate the accuracy of their rankings. They supported their rankings by thoroughly describing the basis for them, by making as much use as possible of available "hard" data to bolster their rankings and conclusions, and by presenting sufficient case study data to allow readers to make their own rankings, if they wished, as a validity check.

Thus, the dependent variable—conflict in educational decision-making—was measured by developing rankings (on the basis of analyses of case study data, including voting behavior in school board elections and tax and bond referenda) of the districts studied on the *incidence* and on the *intensity* of the conflict they experienced during the five year period, 1964-1969, for which data were collected. From these two rankings, an average or overall conflict ranking was established for use as a point of departure for further analysis.

It is important to note, however, that the key findings of the present study do not in fact rely upon the precise rank ordering of the districts, but only upon our ability (1) to demonstrate that we have correctly categorized the districts as relatively "high" or "low" on overall conflict, and (2) to show that the deviant districts—despite the factors which seemed to account for their deviancy—shared the general pattern of political culture apparent in the nondeviant cases.

Data on participation and conflict in each district were collected by means of interviews with the principal participants (such as school board members, superintendents, and citizens active in school affairs) and by means of a review of the minutes of school board meetings and newspaper coverage (where applicable) for the period of time studied, which was set as the five year period from the annual school board election in April 1964 to the election in April 1969. An interview schedule was developed which contained sets of questions designed to elicit data on the key variables determined by the theoretical framework. One area of emphasis in the interviews, and a major means by which the dimensions of conflict, participation by citizens, and school board and superintendent behavior were explored, was the pursuit of detailed descriptions of behavior during the principal issues and controversies each district had experienced. Eight to ten respondents (five to six of the seven school board members in each district, the superintendent, and two to three citizen leaders) were interviewed in each district during 1969 and 1970, with the individual interviews averaging about two hours each. In addition, several followup interviews of shorter duration were held with the superintendent and other key respondents in each district.

The distribution and exercise of "power" and influence within the school district communities—and their effects upon citizen participation and conflict—were investigated both by the collection and analysis of data on actual participation in significant issues by individuals and groups, and by an attempt to assess the possible effects of what Bachrach and Baratz (1962) term the "mobilization of bias" upon the emergence of latent issues. Clearly, if potential issues are being effectively suppressed, this will tend to reduce the level of public conflict.[15] By adopting this two-pronged approach we endeavored to take account of the covert as well as overt effects of the distribution and exercise of power and influence within the school districts studied.[16]

Finally, in an attempt to ascertain the amount of variance in the incidence and intensity of conflict associated with certain features of community social structure identified and emphasized by the literature on community conflict, we employed the following indicators of three structural categories suggested by Gamson (1966):

Structural strain, which refers to tensions arising from change in the community which may lead to conflict, was measured by the magnitude of variation in school district average daily attendance (A.D.A.) and assessed valuation over the decade from 1959 to 1969.[17]

Structural conduciveness to conflict, which refers to structural features which could provide potential lines of cleavage in the community, was measured by the extent to which the school districts possessed distinct solidary groups (such as religious or ethnic groups). Following Gamson's method, groups within the districts were classified as distinct solidary groups if over half of the respondents interviewed mentioned them and attributed to them some common outlook.[18] Districts were ranked on the number and degree of solidarity of solidary groups, the latter dimension being determined according to four criteria suggested by Gamson (1966: 72-73).

Structural integration refers to the extent to which the districts possessed networks of interlocking and cross-cutting ties, both formal (organizational) and informal, which might tend to bind inhabitants together and constrain and inhibit their behavior in issues and affairs of community concern. This was measured indirectly, insofar as possible, by gathering data on the number of local organizations, the extent of their activity and the level of citizen participation within them, and the extent to which they were district-wide and broadly representative in their membership.

According to Gamson's theoretical framework, the three categories of determinants—strain, conduciveness, and integration—are highly interrelated and operate only in conjunction to predict the likelihood and level of conflict a community may experience. For example, "high conduciveness will not produce rancorous conflict if unaccompanied by strain nor if, although accompanied by strain, structural integration is great" (Gamson, 1966: 71).

We shall begin our discussion of the findings with an assessment of the conflict levels in the school districts. This assessment provides the basis for the subsequent analysis in terms of the effects on conflict of community social structure and community normative structure. An analysis of the deviant cases then leads us to the conclusions and research and policy implications of the study.

FINDINGS

OVERALL CONFLICT

The first step in our analysis involved ranking the districts—on the basis of case study data—on the incidence and intensity of conflict experienced.[19] From these rankings, which proved to be highly correlated, we derived an average or overall conflict ranking which is presented in Table 2 along with cumulative voting data for the eight districts. Since the overall conflict ranking is consistent with the initial categorization of the districts according to the status-conflict typology (see Figure 1), our original method of selecting the district is supported. Moreover, the rather strong correlation (shown in Figure 2) between the ranking on overall

TABLE 2
Cumulative Voting Data for the Eight Districts Ranked According to Overall Conflict[a]

District	Type	Total Eligible Voters[b]	Mean % Election Participation	Mean % Election Dissent	Mean % Referendum Participation	Mean % Referendum Dissent	Number of Ref. Held[c] 1964-1969	Number of Ref. Lost[c] 1964-1969
1. Alton	IV	14,800	13.4	38.0	18.3	65.0	2 (2)	2 (2)
2. Weston	IV	12,000	20.0	32.7	17.2	53.2	5 (7)	3 (5)
3. Camden	II	20,000	9.2	13.9	33.8	59.6	7 (11)	4 1/2 (8)
4. Greenwood	II	5,500	5.8	6.5	33.6	44.0	5 (8)	1 1/3 (2)
5. Trenton	III	8,000	14.1	29.3	9.4	45.4	2 (3)	1 (1)
6. Smithville	III	14,000	9.7	14.8	15.7	34.9	1 (1)	0
7. Oakton	I	15,500	7.8	19.9	25.0	33.3	2 (5)	0
8. Northview	I	6,400	3.4	5.2	14.8	19.3	3 (5)	0

[a]The ranking is from highest to lowest in overall conflict. The data are proportions of participation by eligible voters in school board elections and in tax rate and bond referenda for the five year period, 1964-1969, and proportions of total votes which were cast for losers in board elections and against tax rate increases or bond issues during the same time period.

[b]Derived from 1960 U.S. Census data.

[c]The total number of propositions placed before the voters in the various referenda and the total number defeated are given in the numbers within the **parentheses.**

Note: All the districts except Weston and Trenton employed nominating caucuses.

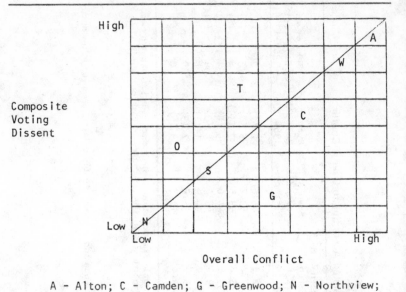

A - Alton; C - Camden; G - Greenwood; N - Northview;
O - Oakton; S - Smithville; T - Trenton; W - Weston

Figure 2: RELATIONSHIP OF RANKINGS ON OVERALL CONFLICT AND
COMPOSITE VOTING DISSENT

conflict and the ranking on composite voting dissent (derived by averaging mean and median percentage voting dissent rankings) tends to validate Minar's use of aggregate voting dissent as an indicator of more generalized conflict in school district policymaking. This is an important point because it provides some degree of confidence that Minar's finding—in his study (1966a) of voting behavior in 48 Chicago suburban school districts—that lower status districts tend to have higher levels of conflict than higher status districts is generalizable for Chicago suburbia as a whole. If this is true, as there appears reason to believe, then we in turn may presume that the patterns of political behavior and conflict which emerge from the data of our nondeviant cases are likely to be typical of higher and lower status Chicago suburban school districts.

This phase of our analysis also revealed that in both the higher and lower status districts the principal issues producing conflict—identified by respondents and by a review of school board minutes and newspaper coverage—included a range of substantive matters (such as the locations of new schools, changes of school attendance boundaries, educational philosophy, and desegregation) that went beyond simply those primarily related to economic considerations. Indeed, in only one of the districts

(Weston) were a majority of the issues clearly related to cost factors. Thus, it appeared that much of the conflict in the lower as well as the higher status districts derived from considerations other than simply the ability or willingness to pay for educational services.

SOCIAL STRUCTURE AND CONFLICT

In the second phase of our analysis we wished to compare the deviant and nondeviant districts and the high and low conflict districts in order to see whether systematic differences in features of their social structures might account for their respective levels of conflict. We were rather surprised to find that rankings on the variables selected as indicators of structural strain, conduciveness, and integration proved to be unreliable predictors of overall conflict, whether taken individually or in combination according to Gamson's (1966) theory (see Table 3). In comparing the high and low conflict nondeviant cases (Types I and IV), for example, while Northview's conflict ranking matches our expectations based on Gamson's theory, Alton—given its low level of growth—and Weston—given its low ranking on conduciveness—should rank lower in conflict. Similarly, Oakton's high ranking on growth (that is, 290% in average daily attendance as compared to Alton's growth of 17% for the same period) seemed to have no bearing on its level of conflict.

Turning to a comparison of the low status deviant and nondeviant cases (Types III and IV), we see that Trenton and Smithville—which rank high on strain and conduciveness and low on integration—ought to rank high on conflict according to Gamson's theory. At the same time, Alton and Weston are the most conflictual districts despite Alton's low level of

TABLE 3
Rankings and Ratings of Districts on Overall Conflict, Growth, Solidary Groups, and Strength and Scope of Organizational Networks

District	Type	Overall Conflict	Growth in A.D.A. & Assessed Valuation (Strain)	Number and Degree of Solidarity of Solidary Groups (Conduciveness)	Strength and Scope of Organizational Networks (Integration)
Alton	IV	1 High	7 Low	2 High	5 Low
Weston	IV	2 High	2 High	6 Low	6 Low
Camden	II	3 High	5 Med.	4 Med.	3 High
Greenwood	II	4 Med.	6 Med.	7 Low	2 High
Trenton	III	5 Med.	4 Med.	1 High	8 Low
Smithville	III	6 Low	3 High	3 High	7 Low
Oakton	I	7 Low	1 High	5 Low	4 Med.
Northview	I	8 Low	8 Low	8 Low	1 High

strain and Weston's low level of conduciveness. Significantly, although Alton and Weston rank above Trenton and Smithville in the strength and scope of their organizational networks (our measure of integration), this feature is associated with *more,* rather than *less,* overall conflict. Indeed, for reasons we shall discuss below, our findings suggest that there may be a tendency in lower status districts for organizational resources to be utilized to *mobilize,* rather than to *suppress,* conflict.

A comparison of the high status deviant and nondeviant cases (Types I and II) again reveals inconsistencies vis-a-vis Gamson's theory. Oakton ranks high on strain while Greenwood ranks low on conduciveness; both Greenwood and Camden rank high on integration. In sum, we are unable to account for variation in conflict levels between deviant and nondeviant and low and high conflict districts on the basis of variation in selected structural features. This result, of course, may be due to the utilization of only a few somewhat imprecise indicators of the structural categories suggested by Gamson.[20] It could also be due to the fact that half of our districts were selected as *deviant* cases; and, although Gamson's theory presents no basis for anticipating exceptions, it is true that our deviant cases provide all but one of the inconsistencies with regard to the expected relationships between conflict levels and the rankings on structural conduciveness and integration. Nevertheless, to the extent that the indicators chosen are representative of their structural categories, the fact that they neither individually nor in combination reliably "predict" the level of conflict experienced suggests that we need to look elsewhere for much of the explanation we seek.[21]

POLITICAL CULTURE AND CONFLICT

In the comparative analysis of the case study data assembled, two variables—leadership by the school authorities and political culture—appeared to account for most of the variation in conflict levels. Taking the latter variable first, among both the districts selected as "deviant" and as "nondeviant" cases, striking and systematic differences in political behavior were clearly apparent. These seemed to flow from differing political cultures in, on the one hand, the higher status, predominantly white-collar districts and, on the other hand, the lower status, predominantly blue-collar districts. The existence of distinctive political cultures—and hence differing community normative structures—was indicated both by extensive data linking the differences in political behavior to norms, attitudes, and values concerning the conduct of politics, and by the nature of the systematic patterns of behavior, which conformed to behavior associated with what Banfield and Wilson (1963) describe as the *public-regarding* and *private-regarding* political cultures.

Banfield and Wilson contend that the various social cleavages in American cities and metropolitan areas tend to coalesce into two basic opposing patterns (or political cultures) deriving from the "fundamental cleavage between the public-regarding, Anglo-Saxon Protestant, middle-class ethos and the private-regarding, lower-class, immigrant ethos" (1963: 40). These culturally-based orientations spring from more than simply differences in social class and affluence. The public-regarding political culture emphasizes the values of the Reform Movement, that is, efficiency, "good government," and the disinterested support of the broad public interest. By contrast, the private-regarding culture, which is associated with "machine" politics, seeks personal benefits and favors from the political system and identifies with the ward or neighborhood rather than the community as a whole. While the private-regarding culture recognizes the legitimacy of competition and conflict between groups concerned with narrow and special interests, the public-regarding culture takes "the view that politics, rather than being a struggle among partial and private interests is (or at any rate ought to be) a disinterested effort to discover what is best for the community 'as a whole' " (1963: 154). Banfield and Wilson argue that the dominance of one ethos over the other gives rise to distinctive patterns of style, structure, and policies in local politics.[22]

As the short description above suggests, these two political cultures tend to produce different types of citizen participation which are likely to affect the incidence and intensity of conflict. Indeed, this proved to be the case in the blue-collar and white-collar districts studied. Thus, in relation to theories of participation and conflict, a rather surprising finding of the study was that, in terms of conflict, the *type* of citizen participation was more important than the *volume* of participation, the dimension of participation which has traditionally received the most attention.[23]

Minar, in his explanation of the differing levels of conflict in white-collar and blue-collar districts (1966b: 8), has emphasized the importance in their respective political cultures of the distinctive norms and values associated with their differential possession of resources of "conflict management skills" (that is, "perspectives and experiences that prize specialization, division of labor, delegation of authority, and technical expertise," thus affecting the way they conduct public business). However, the findings of the present study indicate that a satisfactory explanation of the incidence of conflict must also take explicit account of their norms and values concerning the nature of *politics* itself—in other words, the norms and values at the heart of their respective political cultures. While on the basis of the data we certainly agree with Minar about the importance of conflict management resources, we believe that they represent only half, and probably not the most significant half, of an adequate explanation of the differences in the incidence and intensity of conflict in blue-collar and white-collar suburban school districts. In other words, if as Minar (1966b: 133) recognizes, "the application of these conflict management skills reflects (a) their availability in the community context, and (b) community expectations as to the means and ends of doing public business," then the nature of these community expectations becomes a vital part of a complete explanation of the variance observed in political behavior. This point becomes more apparent when one recognizes that the organizational and management skills of citizens can be, and not infrequently are, utilized to mobilize political opposition and aggravate conflict rather than to minimize conflict and maximize support for the authorities.[24]

To summarize our position, we agree, on the basis of the data, that the availability of management resources clearly has a great deal to do with the *structuring* of the political process of school district governance. The crucial "rules of the game" affecting the process, however, appear to derive more from the cultural ethos than from perspectives associated with the level of management resources available. According to Banfield and Wilson's description of their "ethos theory," the "rules of the game" which differentiate the public and private-regarding political cultures appear to vary along four major dimensions:

(1) the extent to which competition and "politics" are viewed as legitimate,

(2) the extent to which the public interest is defined in terms of the whole community,

(3) the extent to which honesty, impartiality, and disinterested participation are expected, and

(4) the extent to which efficiency and expertise in governance are valued.[25]

In order to support these conclusions, we will now present a summary of the data pertaining to the above dimensions. Following this, we will discuss our analysis of the "deviant" cases which helps clarify the relationship to conflict levels of aggregate management resources, norms and values concerning "politics" (that is, political culture), and the quality of leadership provided by the school authorities.

The Legitimacy of Competition and "Politics"

Although the populaces of both the white-collar and blue-collar districts accepted and professed the view that politics should be "kept out" of education, there was a significant difference in terms of the general attitude toward, and meaning ascribed to, "politics," as well as in what went on in practice. While in the white-collar districts "politics" was shunned as unseemly, unnecessary, and improper because it was believed a common interest could and should be defined, in the blue-collar districts competing interests and points of view tended to be an accepted fact of life. In the latter districts, keeping politics out of education chiefly meant that political parties should not interfere in school affairs and that the administration and governance of education should be free of patronage and corruption. Such occurrences were virtually unheard of in the white-collar districts. The emphasis on these points in the blue-collar districts, however, was more than theoretical. In at least one of the districts, payoffs and patronage were not entirely things of the past. In the others, "machine" style political behavior and periodic revelations of corruption in municipal or township government were a constant reminder of the dangers of the coarser side of politics. Unlike the white-collar districts, in three out of four of the blue-collar districts political parties (often nominally "nonpartisan") were judged to be the most important local organizations and appeared to reach a larger proportion of the inhabitants than any other organizations.

Although overt activity in education on the part of local political parties and politicians was rare in both white-collar and blue-collar districts, informal and indirect linkages between the school systems and the local political parties tended to be much more important in the blue-collar districts, mainly in terms of the recruitment of school board members. In the absence of effective nonpartisan structures for the recruitment and support of board members, blue-collar school boards were inclined to be self-recruiting and often turned to local politicians and political parties in seeking new board members. This practice was reflected in the fact that three out of four of the blue-collar districts had persons on their school boards who were also active in leadership roles in local political organizations. This state of affairs was not found to be the case in any of the white-collar districts, where influence tended to be concentrated in local civic organizations rather than in local political parties.[26]

The preeminence of the political parties in the blue-collar districts seemed accountable to the traditions and values of their citizens, large numbers of whom are foreign born or first generation Americans. In part, the parties appeared to be supported in order to protect and enhance the interest of groups and community areas within the districts. In part, the popularity of the parties seemed to flow from an approach to politics as a form of "play," as an enjoyable diversion and sport (see Banfield and Wilson, 1963: 22). Interview data suggesting this attitude included descriptions of the boisterious character of citizen participation in political parties and political clubs and of the interest and fascination commanded by community controversies. For example, during a teachers' strike in Weston, citizens turned out in droves to attend the heated negotiations between the teachers' union and the school board which were open to the public and were described as being "more entertaining than television." Another manifestation of this attitude toward politics may be found in the response of a blue-collar school board member, who, when asked why he served on the board, said, "I looked on it initially as a form of recreation, a hobby, and I still see it this way to some extent. It's interesting and less expensive than bowling." The data indicate that, as a result of this attitude toward politics, hotly contested school board elections in blue-collar districts were rather widely enjoyed rather than being viewed as a sort of social disaster, as such elections tended to be perceived when, on occasion, they occurred in white-collar districts.

The norms against political competition and conflict in white-collar districts can be illustrated by two examples. In Northview, the formation and activity or a self-appointed citizens group critical of the school system (the first such group in the history of the district) was greeted with an icy response from the public, despite the fact that it was admitted in private that the group had identified many legitimate problems. It was felt that this "just wasn't the way to go about things," that is, to seek change, especially since the incumbent superintendent was near retirement. The group soon began to disintegrate as its members responded to the cues they were receiving. Eventually, several members of the group worked their way up to leadership positions within the school district "establishment." Similarly, in Greenwood, when a controversy led to a situation in which two independent candidates decided to run for the school board in competition with the slate of candidates endorsed by the district nominating caucus, the independent candidates—who were not aligned—felt called upon to publicly apologize for and justify their decision to challenge the caucus, since their action was virtually unprecedented. By contrast, in Alton, a blue-collar district employing a caucus, independent candidates regularly ran against the caucus slate and no need was seen for any apology for this.

The functioning as well as the existence of nominating caucuses to select school board candidates—which in the Chicago suburbs appears much more likely to occur in white-collar than in blue-collar districts (see Minar, 1966a: 829-831)—seems accountable to cultural values vis-a-vis politics as well as to the level of management resources available. Indeed, caucuses of this type appear to be inventions of the middle-class reform movement and are often associated with nonpartisan systems (Banfield and Wilson, 1963: 143). The avowed purposes of caucuses appear to be very public-regarding ones. Caucuses are said to exist as mechanisms for seeking the best qualified persons available for school board service and they operate on the assumption that "the job should seek the man" rather than vice versa. While it could be easily argued that it would be more democratic for the caucuses to offer the voters a choice between several well-qualified candidates, in practice the caucuses in white-collar Chicago suburban districts overwhelmingly choose to present the voters with single slates of candidates. These typically run unopposed (see Minar, 1966a: 829-831), a procedure and response which may be more accountable to a desire to avoid political competition and conflict than to the inexorable workings of the plentiful management resources of white-collar districts. As one of the white-collar school board member respondents put it, "the whole point of the caucus is to *avoid* having to run for office," an undertaking which he went on to indicate was viewed as onerous, immodest, and potentially embarassing. In contrast to the white-collar districts, the few blue-collar districts which employ caucuses are more likely to face opposition from independent candidates (Minar, 1966a: 829-831), a fact which may be as much a result of cultural values as of a deficiency of managerial resources. The fact that the caucus nominees in white-collar districts are typically unopposed accounts not only for the low levels of electoral *conflict* in these districts, but also for their low levels of electoral *participation* in settings where one would otherwise expect high levels because of the "participativeness" associated with higher status populaces.

Honesty, Impartiality, and Disinterested Participation

While the moderately to highly affluent citizens of the white-collar districts studied for the most part had little or nothing to gain in the way of *material* personal benefits from their school systems, and, further, professed or accepted an ideology which prohibited such self-seeking, the same was not true of many of the citizens of the blue-collar districts studied.[27] Interview data from blue-collar district board members and superintendents indicated that board members tended to both expect and to receive requests for favors from their constituents, and that some members tried to grant these requests toward the end of building their political following. In particular, school board members frequently mentioned receiving personal requests from citizens for custodial or other noncertified positions for themselves, their friends, or relatives. Further, board members in three out of four of the blue-collar districts alluded to the days in the not too distant past when noncertified positions in their systems were objects of patronage. Indeed, in Weston one of the largest controversies in fact involved allegations against the school board concerning the use of custodians jobs as "political plums," reputed "ghosts" on the district's payroll, and suspicion of bribery in the case of the retention of an attorney. The majority of this particular board, which became completely discreditied, was also accused of holding secret "bootleg" board meetings at which they plotted their machinations. Interestingly, in regard to "explaining" observed political behavior, a subsequent "reform" member of this board remarked that he felt that the competitiveness of board elections and the greater turnout of voters for board elections than for referenda in his district was at least partly accountable to the tradition of patronage associated with the board.

The history of patronage and occasional revelations of corruption in local government, and in a few cases in the school systems themselves, tended to make the residents of blue-collar districts supicious of public officials, including both school administrators and school board members. Three out of four of the blue-collar districts studied had had scandals in local government within the past decade. One of the districts, already alluded to, had also unquestionably had cases of improper behavior involving school authorities. On the other hand, none of the white-collar districts in the study had such histories to undermine trust in public officials. Thus, the reluctance to delegate authority and to defer to expertise common in the blue-collar districts derived not only from the paucity of managerial experiences and attitudes in the populace but also from aspects of the political culture which generated suspicion of public officials.

The Broad Public Interest

In general, in the blue-collar districts there was a greater allegiance to subcommunities and groups within the districts than to what was "best" for the *whole* school system. This tendency was often aggravated by the fact that three out of four of the districts subsumed several villages or communities within their boundaries. Although the same was true of two of the four white-collar districts, in these districts potential lines of cleavage seldom interfered with the pursuit of the "best interest" of the whole school district. These points are illustrated by the fact that while in the white-collar districts the PTAs tended to work together well to promote projects, including referenda, to benefit the whole district, there was a notable lack of unity among the PTAs within the blue-collar districts. This lack of unity was clearly partly accountable to the pronounced allegiance, apparent in both actions and words, of blue-collar PTAs to their own school and subcommunities. At the same time, insufficient managerial and leadership skills and the general weakness of the PTAs themselves in the blue-collar districts, were also factors which contributed to the lack of unity.

Other evidence suggesting allegiance to subcommunities and groups in the blue-collar districts included aspects of voting behavior and the performance of school board members. The citizens of the blue-collar districts manifested certain of their "attachments" in the phenomenon of "name-voting," a practice not detected in the white-collar districts. In all four of the blue-collar districts, respondents volunteered that having a name associated with certain ethnic groups would attract votes in board elections. As one board member put it, "Being Bohemian will draw votes; being Bohemian and Catholic is even better." In the case of the performance of board members, although the board members in all the districts studied are elected at-large, those in the blue-collar districts appeared more inclined than their counterparts in the white-collar districts to represent and serve the interests of subcommunities or areas within their districts.

Finally, the difference between the blue-collar and white-collar districts in terms of their ideology regarding the definition of the public interest can be depicted in the manner in which competing demands were presented. When, on occasion, the consensus regarding what was "best" for the whole district broke down in the white-collar districts (and, of course, this happened most frequently in the "deviant" white-collar districts), there was a tendency for competing views to be couched in the rhetoric of "the broad public interest" even when in substance they clearly reflected the desires of subcommunities or special interest groups. On the other hand, in the blue-collar districts, demands generally were simply presented from a neighborhood or subcommunity point of view with little or no attempt to justify them in terms of what was "best" for the whole district. The former pattern occurred, for example, in Greenwood during a controversy over the site for a new junior high. Neighborhood groups near the old junior high argued that a nearby vacant lot on which they feared an apartment building might be constructed (to the detriment of their neighborhood, as they saw it) was the "best" site, despite the fact that a larger and more conveniently situated lot nearer the old school was preferred by the school authorities and their architects. By contrast, during a controversy in Alton over the adjustment of school attendance area boundaries to equalize class size, neighborhood groups simply demanded the restoration of their former neighborhood school patterns, although they knew this would recreate overcrowding problems in some schools.

So far, we have shown that our data strongly suggest that differences in *both* the political culture and management resources of white-collar and blue-collar districts lead to different types of citizen participation and political behavior, which in turn tend to cause predictable differences in the incidence and intensity of conflict in school politics. Since the systematic differences in political culture from higher to lower status districts were readily apparent in deviant as well as nondeviant cases, we are left with the problem of explaining the failure of the deviant cases to "behave," with regard to conflict levels, in the manner expected on the basis of our theoretical analysis.[28]

ANALYSIS OF DEVIANT CASES

In their comparative analyses of the four school districts they studied in collaboration, Minar (1966b) and Snow (1966, 1967) found that the quality of leadership by school authorities seemed to account for much of the variance in conflict levels not readily attributable to contextual factors, such as the availability of management resources. The same was true in the present study. As compared with the high status/low conflict districts (Northview and Oakton), many of the difficulties of the high status/ high conflict districts (Greenwood and Camden) seemed to stem from naive, unrealistic, or unresourceful leadership behavior with regard to school and community relations by their authorities.[29] On the other hand, as compared with the low status/high conflict districts (Alton and Weston), astute and enterprising leadership by the authorities in the low status/low conflict districts (Trenton and Smithville) appeared to partially offset their many contextual disadvantages and contribute to their relatively low conflict levels. Finally, although there were numerous and frequently important differences among the eight districts, the four districts lowest on overall conflict appeared generally to have more resourceful leadership from their authorities than did the four districts highest on overall conflict, three of which witnessed provocative behavior by their authorities which intensified or precipitated conflict.

It would, of course, be simplistic and farfetched to suggest that more effective leadership by the authorities in itself could have brought the high conflict districts down to the conflict levels of the low conflict districts when many other variables than the quality of leadership obviously were involved. However, it does appear that in many instances conflict might have been appreciably reduced by more resourceful leadership. In particular, in the comparative analysis two dimensions of leadership seemed to be especially important: politically sensitive behavior (as opposed to apolitical behavior), and proactive behavior to retain the initiative (as opposed to reactive behavior in which the authorities tend to be on the defensive). Because of space limitations, we shall have to confine ourselves to a brief summary of the data supporting these conclusions, focusing for illustrative purposes on two of the four deviant cases.[30]

To begin with the high status/high conflict cases, Greenwood provides a striking example of the effects of unrealistic and apolitical leadership behavior. Greenwood is remarkably similar to Northview (the district lowest on overall conflict) in terms of the composition of its population, its size, and its advantageous resources and structural features. But the Greenwood school board precipitated a crisis by ignoring the recommendation of a citizens advisory committee it had appointed to consider the question of whether the district should enlarge its existing junior high or build a new middle school. Four members of the citizens committee opposed the board's decision to build a new school and formed an ad hoc group of about 40 citizens which very skillfully fought the necessary bond referendum, which was defeated. Board members interviewed stated, in retrospect, that they had realized that their decision might not be popular in some quarters, but that they had counted on majority support for their bond referendum because they were convinced that it was in the "best" interest of the district from an *educational* standpoint. However, although cost was not a factor in this affluent suburb—as demonstrated by the fact that the voters approved a school tax rate increase included on the same ballot with the ill-fated bond referendum—it is apparent from our data that at the time of the issue a number of values in addition to educational ones (such as convenience of location) were being weighed by large segments of the populace.

In the aftermath of the referendum defeat, with both the consensus concerning what was "best" for the district and the local norms against conflict temporarily shattered, the school board groped for a solution to the junior high issue. They next proposed a bond referendum to authorize an addition to the the existing junior high, but this proposal became embroiled in a new dispute over which property adjacent to the existing school should be utilized. Again, the board had chosen to disregard the advice and requests of citizens involved—this time on a self-appointed basis—in favor of doing what it thought was best *educationally;* again many of these citizens joined together to organize an effective ad hoc opposition group. Following the defeat of the second referendum, the board capitulated and delegated the resolution of the issue to a new citizens advisory committee made up of opponents and proponents of the previous referenda. The "compromise" referendum proposal which emerged, and which was successfully passed, simply revised the second proposal to satisfy citizens' demands regarding the property to be utilized.[31]

The intense controversy which Greenwood experienced was certainly not brought about by any deficiency in management resources—either in the populace or on the school board, which was loaded with executives—or by a lack of general commitment to public-regarding values. Nor did the controversy seem to spring from ideological differences within the community, which was the case in the instance of Camden (the other high status/high conflict district), where much of the conflict derived from a fundamental ideological clash—exacerbated by inept behavior on the part of the school authorities—between advocates of conservative and liberal educational and governmental philosophies. However, it did appear that the unrealistic and apolitical behavior of the Greenwood school board— ironically derived from an *excess* of public-regarding zeal for what it thought could be demonstrated to be "best" for the district—triggered the conflict by destroying (temporarily) the credibility of the assumption of a *single* public interest upon which the public-regarding cluture rests.[32] In Camden, on the other hand, ideological differences within the populace made a public-regarding consensus regarding the school system difficult to maintain despite widespread lip service to this value.

Moving now to the low status/low conflict districts, Smithville and Trenton had in common astute leadership and a distribution of the electorate within their boundaries which enabled the largest subcommunity in each district to control district decision-making, an accomplishment which was facilitated by the presence of a single dominant local political party in each district.[33] Both of these subcommunities consistently utilized the voting advantage they enjoyed to dominate district affairs toward the end of protecting their own interests, not the least of which was to try to maintain the separation existing between themselves and all-black subcommunities within the districts.

In Trenton the situation in several important respects resembled that described by Vidich and Bensman (1958) in their celebrated study of "Springdale." Like Mr. Peabody in Springdale, Trenton's superintendent operated under heavy constraints imposed by an uncooperative school board dominated by a very conservative subcommunity. Like Mr. Peabody, the superintendent nevertheless exerted what appeared to be the maximum possible influence, under the circumstances, by means of full and strategic use of his limited resources. For example, to contend with the lack of deference from his all-blue-collar board, their propensity to meddle in routine administrative matters, and their inclination to caucus informally prior to meetings to decide how they would vote on certain matters, the superintendent intentionally made the agendas he sent out in advance of board meetings as sketchy as possible and then allowed the board to bog down whenever it liked in "administrivia." This approach tended to leave open to the superintendent the opportunity to move ahead somewhat independently, in a quiet and cautious fashion, in such substantive areas as curriculum development. Again, like Mr. Peabody, the superintendent knew his community and made maximum use of the rather weak

PTAs as support organizations, for example in getting out the vote for referenda the board had approved but for which it had done little campaigning.

In sum, however, as much as the superintendent's skills contributed to the reduction of conflict, it was the combination of his leadership with the strong dominance of the main subcommunity (together with the dominant local political party which structured this power and acted, as in Smithville, as a conflict reducing mechanism) that appeared to account for the moderate level of overall conflict in a setting which otherwise might have produced intense conflict.[34]

CONCLUSIONS AND IMPLICATIONS

COMMUNITY STRUCTURE AND CONFLICT

If it is safe to assume, as suggested by Minar's study (1966a) of 48 districts and by our findings, that high status districts tend to be low on conflict and low status districts tend to be high on conflict, the present study suggests that, at least in the Chicago suburban area, this is due both to differences in political culture and in the level of management resources. It appears that in "normal" cases, higher status districts will tend to have public-regarding cultures (which tend to lead to harmony and the avoidance of conflict) as well as plentiful management resources, while lower status districts will tend to have private-regarding cultures (which tend to lead to tension and conflict) coupled with meager management resources. In "deviant" cases, the public-regarding tendency toward consensus of high status/high conflict districts will have broken down, most likely because of ideological tensions and/or as a result of inept leadership, and management resources will be used to mobilize conflict. Low status/low conflict districts may exist as a result of unusually skilled leadership behavior by the authorities and/or as a consequence of a distribution or control (perhaps through the existence of political machines) of power within the districts which tends to suppress conflict.

As well as having *direct* effects on conflict levels, our data suggest that the normative structure of communities also has significant *indirect* effects through its impact on aspects of community social structure. In other words, although our indicators of selected features of the social structure proved by themselves to be poor predictors of the level of overall conflict a district experienced, our case study data suggest that certain of these features were nevertheless of considerable importance in terms of conflict, their status and effects being influenced by the political culture of the community and their consequences moderated by the factors which seemed to account for the deviancy of the atypical districts. Thus, whether districts were deviant or not, there was more consciousness of real or potential parochial divisions (increasing structural conduciveness) and more allegiance to these divisions (weakening structural integration) in private-regarding districts than in public-regarding ones. For example, in the latter ethnic identity was muted and considerably less important in social relationships than in the former. More broadly, as compared with the private-regarding districts, heterogeneity in the public-regarding districts was less likely to be translated into *socially significant* as opposed to simply *demographic* divisions within the community.[35] Still more important, there was considerable evidence that existing divisions in private-regarding districts had more potent consequences for conflict than divisions extant in public-regarding districts, where the ethos tended to reduce both their saliency and the legitimacy of political action on their behalf. Indeed, it appeared that a community's normative structure set the terms for the action of the integrative and disintegrative features of community social structure. In sum, our analysis leads us to propose for further investigation the propositions: (1) that the more private-regarding a community, the greater will be its structural conduciveness, the weaker will be its structural integration, and—other things being equal (as in nondeviant cases)—the higher will be its level of conflict; and (2) that the more public-regarding a community, the less will be its structural conduciveness, the greater will be its instructural integration, and—*ceteris paribus*—the lower will be its level of conflict.

PATTERNS OF POLITICAL CULTURE

Because our study included a sample of only eight suburban school districts in one metropolitan area, the significance our our findings regarding the presence of distinctive patterns of political culture and their consequences for school politics and community conflict clearly depends, first, on the extent to which these patterns are representative of those generally found in predominantly white-collar and predominantly blue-collar Chicago suburban communities and, second, upon the extent to which these patterns are found in suburban communities of the same types in *other* metropolitan areas.[36] Although further research is needed on both points, we are inclined to believe that our findings are representative of "white-collar" and "blue-collar" Chicago suburban school districts for the reasons enumerated earlier. In addition, a secondary analysis of the data collected by O'Shea (1971) in his study of 15 Chicago suburban school districts is also supportive of our conclusions.

The extent to which these patterns of political culture are found in white-collar and blue-collar suburban communities in other metropolitan areas is more problematic. Further research is particularly needed in metropolitan areas that, unlike Chicago, are not known for a central city tradition of machine politics. It may be that such a tradition—and the private-regarding culture which it implies and tends to reinforce—is necessary to produce, through socialization and migration, workingclass suburbs in which there is a carryover of private-regardingness. On the other hand, Wilson and Banfield's rather controversial "political ethos theory"[37] — which they have recently (1971) revised and refined—indicates that ethnicity and social class are the key variables differentiating those associated with the two political cultures. Thus, the presence of an active political machine, or of the residual effects of one comparatively recently demised, might not be necessary conditions for the presence of private-regardiness. This is an important point since relatively few political machines resembling the old type now exist, and since, according to Banfield and Wilson (1963: 329-346), the trend of city politics—with the ever increasing absorbtion of lower-class, immigrant groups into the middle class—has been and is more and more toward the public-regarding values of the reform movement, which, they contend the Protestant elite in America has established as the norm for the middle class.

Although we must await the verdict of further research concerning the significance of political culture in suburban school politics and community conflict, an analysis (Boyd, 1973) of major problem areas associated with the original version of the ethos theory suggests some directions for future research. In particular, it appears that a broader approach may be needed than might have seemed appropriate from a narrow interpretation of the original theory. Because there is reason to suspect that social class may be more important than ethnicity as a determinant of political culture, it appears that research is needed in metropolitan areas both *high* and *low* in the proportion of immigrant ethnic groups in their populaces, as well as in metropolitan areas *with* and *without* reformed governments in their central cities. Future research should be especially sensitive to the effects of the working class subculture upon political orientation, and to the possible differences in political culture between the middle and upper middle class. (On these points see Wilson and Banfield, 1971; and Gans, 1962: 229-278.)[38]

NONPARTISANSHIP AND CONFLICT MANAGEMENT IN SCHOOL GOVERNANCE

At the outset, we noted that research has shown that high levels of conflict tend to reduce the autonomy of school administrators and also frequently have a debilitating effect on both school superintendents and school board members. Our findings, which are consistent with these propositions, suggest that the difficulties of school authorities in managing conflict stem in large part from the nature of the *nonpartisan* system, the nature of the populace served, and the nature of the professional and political ideologies of educators.

To reiterate some of our earlier points, the management of conflict under the nonpartisan system of government (common to most school districts) is accomplished not through maneuvering, bargaining, and compromise among competing interest groups and political parties, but, to a large extent, through the shared conviction that reasonable men deliberating together in pursuit of the broad public interest can—or ought to be able to—achieve consensus without significant or lasting disagreements. This being the case, it is clear that the attitudes, beliefs, communicative skills, and so forth, of the participants are crucial to the success of nonpartisan government. Thus, we found that the political culture and level of management resources available combine to pose some difficult problems for conflict management in blue-collar school districts. Given the greater propensity for organizational participation of higher status than of lower status persons, the white-collar districts studied had considerably stronger and more fully developed networks of local organizations than did the blue-collar districts. This is a very significant point, for the strength of local organizations is a particularly important factor in *nonpartisan* political systems, where these organizations often play a crucial role in the mobilization of support for the authorities.[39] This fact is neatly summed up in the remark of a city manager, quoted by Wood (1959: 184), "God bless all civic associations. They are the city manager's ward machines."

Since the most important local organizations in the blue-collar districts studied were generally political parties rather than civic associations, and the political parties were expected to "stay out" (at least overtly) of school affairs, the effective organizational network that blue-collar school districts could draw upon was still further reduced. Consequently, the school authorities in blue-collar districts had difficulty mobilizing support and were quite vulnerable to organized opposition, when it materialized. Finding their constituents unmoved by the logic of the public-regarding rhetoric which accompanies the nonpartisan system, these authorities, to strengthen their position, were inclined to develop informal linkages with local politicians and political parties, but this rather precarious practice could not realize its full potential because of ironically constraining norms. In this and many other matters, the authorities were forced to contend with the conflict-producing tensions and constraints generated by the contradictory values of their cultural ethos, on the one hand, and the non-partisan system on the other. By contrast, the congruence of the values of the public-regarding culture of the white-collar districts with the values of the nonpartisan system tended to promote something approaching the harmony and efficiency envisioned by the architects of the reform movement. Yet, the school authorities in white-collar districts were also quite vulnerable when the public-regarding tendency toward consensus broke down, because this tended to throw their support structure of civic organizations into disarray.

In light of the impact that even quite small opposition groups can produce in nonpartisan school districts—given the structural and political vulnerability of those polities we have just noted—it would seem that the school authorities should display careful attention and sensitivity to the political realities of the world in which they operate. Yet, all too often the school authorities in the districts studied precipitated or aggravated conflict by politically naive and provocative behavior. Of course, part of their difficulty in attempting to manage conflict stems from the fact that the nonpartisan system leads them to be unused to facing opposition—particularly organized opposition—and, hence, inexperienced in dealing with it. Although school board members, as laymen, can plead "amateur status" in this regard, one might fairly expect school superintendents, as professionals, to provide more sophisticated political leadership in conflict management. It appears, however, that the ideology of professional school administrators that they are "nonpolitical" educational experts often creates problems for them in managing conflict.[40]

To the extent that contemporary school administrators subscribe to the traditional ideology of their profession, their task of conflict management is made more difficult, not only by the hard-dying myth of the non-political nature of educational policymaking, but also by several other aspects of this ideology. Despite occasional platitudes about the separation of policymaking (as a lay citizen responsibility) from administration (as a professional responsibility), within the profession of school administration there seems to be a common belief that school superintendents should play a large role with their school boards in the way of professional leadership in policy development. Thus, superintendents sometimes seem to find themselves deeply implicated in the political accountability associated with policymaking, but unprepared (emotionally and technically) for the political maneuvering necessary for survival.[41] Further, school superintendents tend to feel that they are supposed to provide leadership toward the adoption of the latest and most sophisticated educational techniques and ideas. When one couples this tendency with the middle and upper-middle-class values which many superintendents hold, we find, at best, that their perspectives and preferences are inclined to be somewhat ill-suited to the realities, if not the needs, of lower and working class communities.[42]

To conclude, our findings suggest that there is an inherent tension between the ideal "nonpolitical" model of educational governance advanced by reformers and professional educators and the political culture of blue-collar school districts. To the extent that this is true, and further research in other parts of our country is much needed in this regard, the training and expectations of school administrators who may serve in such districts should be adjusted accordingly, and possibly the system of educational governance itself should be changed. It appears that school superintendents in blue-collar districts—where, because of the cultural ethos and available management resources, there is less deference to expertise than in white-collar districts—are often forced to play the role of pragmatic political strategists while their counterparts in white-collar districts are more often able to play the role of "nonpolitical" educational experts that is more consistent with the ideology of their profession and training. While both roles in fact are political ones—the role of the nonpartisan expert simply relies on a different and more covert brand of politics—school superintendents in blue-collar districts should be less burdened with the constraining baggage of a professional ideology which is ill-suited to their situation and which in some cases, as our data suggest, tends to incapacitate them with role conflict. Finally, there is the possibly unpalatable implication that it might be beneficial to abandon the rather quixotic and Procrustean attempt to fit blue-collar communities to the *nonpartisan* system of educational governance, when and where their cultural ethos would appear to be much more supportive of a *partisan* system.[43] Given the myths and conventional wisdom which surround both education and politics, however, it may well be doubted whether citizens and educators in blue-collar communities would be likely to recognize the advantages which might accrue from such a perverse "reform."

NOTES

1. For discussions of some of the reasons for the belatedness of serious study of educational politics, see Eliot (1959) and Meranto (1970: 1-14).

2. For reviews of the growing literature on school politics, including some of the most important studies of large city school systems, see Kirst (1970: v-16); Kirst and Mosher (1969); Wirt (1970); and Peterson (1974).

3. The 1970 U.S. Census shows that 57% of the total metropolitan population of the United States now resides in suburbia. Thus 37% of the nation's population are suburbanites, as compared to 31% each for city and rural areas.

4. Since many suburbs tend to be relatively homogeneous in terms of social class, as compared to most cities, such suburbs provide opportune research sites for the investigation and comparison of the systematic effects of particular social status levels upon social and political behavior.

5. Note, however, that in an excellent study of suburban school politics, Lyke (1968) found that increased citizen participation did *not* significantly reduce the discretion of school administrators. This discrepancy may be explained by the fact that, as compared with the suburban school districts studied by Minar and by the present author, Lyke's four districts do not appear to be ones that experienced *high* levels of sustained conflict and associated citizen participation.

6. Whether such a process is likely to produce "better," more rational educational policies is, of course, another question entirely.

7. Of course, conflict is not always dysfunctional (Coser, 1956). Indeed, progress frequently requires that conflict be played out. However, better knowledge of the causes and dynamics of conflict may enable leaders to behave in ways which will reduce the likelihood of both unnecessary conflict and intense conflict with traumatic consequences for the community. On this point, see Coleman (1957).

8. While such resources may enable the reduction of the number of issues which arise—through skills in the anticipation of reactions and the design of strategies of conflict avoidance—the general suppression of controversial issues would seem to require additional factors, such as a "mobilization of bias" by powerful community interests to confine the scope of local politics to relatively "safe" issues (Bachrach and Baratz, 1962). All community interests cannot be served equally—even in an affluent suburb (consider, for example, the frequently conflicting interests of "newcomers" and "oldtimers" (see Wood, 1959)—and since many groups in high status suburbs are likely to possess sufficient resources (including management resources) to try to protect and promote their interests, it follows that management resources alone will not be sufficient to generally suppress controversial issues.

9. Note, however, that Minar began the exploration of these questions in his followup study (1966b).

10. For example, scholars have viewed with concern findings suggesting that as compared with higher status populaces, lower status populaces are less committed to democratic norms, more inclined toward authoritarianism, more likely to feel powerless and alienated, and are more susceptible to demagoguery and radical ideologies (Lipset, 1959; Kornhauser, 1959). With respect to the social structure, as noted earlier both the low levels of participation in voluntary associations characteristic of lower status populaces and the less well developed networks of such associations typical of lower status communities have caused concern among theorists; they hold that, by standing between individuals and government, formal organizations perform valuable mediating and moderating functions which reduce the likelihood of conflict (Coleman, 1957; Kornhauser, 1959). However, it should be noted that some theorists (Gusfield, 1962; Crain and Rosenthal, 1967) hold the contrary view that higher levels of citizen participation and activity by voluntary associations may *heighten* rather than *lessen* conflict propensity.

11. However, a deficiency of some studies of community conflict has been their tendency to concentrate mainly upon factors in *either* the normative structure *or* the social structure. For examples, see Gamson (1966) and Minar (1966a).

12. In our use of the term "power structure," we make no presumption that power is likely to be concentrated or dispersed or that the structure is likely to remain constant over time.

13. By way of explanation, according to Easton (1965: 48), *demands* arise when people express the desire that any of their wants be satisfied authoritatively, or demands may arise within the political system itself. For him, demands are "a main point of contention in political life," and "conflicts over demands constitute the flesh and blood of all political systems." Support involves the degree to which people approve of the system that is processing demands for them. The amount of support given to the political system is viewed as the net balance of support, opposition, and indifference.

14. Specifically, the selection procedure was as follows: All 118 districts were ranked from highest to lowest on 1960 median family income. Referenda results were noted for the 35 highest (from $9,200 to $23,065 median family income) and the 45 lowest districts (from $5,130 to $7,999 median family income). Two pairs of districts were selected from the 31 highest and two pairs from the 30 lowest districts. The criterion of conflict chosen seemed reasonably selective since the data showed that only 7 of the 35 high status and 13 of the 45 low status districts qualified as high conflict districts. Since it could be argued that districts with a heavy tax burden and limited financial resources (that is, those with high tax rates and low assessed valuation per pupil) might be more prone to conflict in school politics than districts with a light tax burden and abundant financial resources, it would have been desirable to control for this possibility by selecting for each cell of the design destricts representative of the former and the latter characteristics. However, from among the districts which met the earlier criteria of community status and conflict, the best that could be done was to select two districts (Oakton and Smithville) which possessed high tax rates and low assessed valuation per pupil for the low conflict cells, and one district (Alton) which possessed a low tax rate and high assessed valuation for the high conflict/low status cell. Finally, of the eight districts originally selected, all but one (a high status/high conflict district) agreed to participate in the study. The next high status/high conflict district approached (to replace the one above) readily agreed to participate. Following the usual practice, pseudonyms are used to protect the identity of all participants.

15. Our attempt to assess the undeniably elusive possibilities of a "mobilization of bias" was restricted to an effort (1) to analyze school district policy in terms of "who benefits" and (2) to try to determine to what extent and by what means those benefiting were in a commanding position to protect and maintain their advantages against the disadvantaged.

16. There is, or course, great controversy about the proper means of determining the distribution and exercise of "power" and influence within communities. Some scholars (such as March, 1966) have even raised doubts about the utility of the concept of "power" for research. Moreover, Bachrach and Baratz's concept of the covert uses of power to create what they call "nondecision-making" situations is not without its detractors (see Merelman, 1968; Wolfinger, 1971). However, the utility of the concepts of "power" and "nondecision-making" is being reaffirmed by the recent work of scholars such as Connolly (1974) and Crenson (1971). Thus, we take the pragmatic point of view that the analytical approaches suggested by this voluminous literature (reviewed, for example, by Hawley and Wirt, 1968)—when used in combination and interpreted with care—enable us to gain an important degree of understanding of a vital phase of political life.

17. Previous research (Kirkendall, 1966) had shown that substantial change in school district assessed valuation was an important predictor of subsequent conflict. See also Iannacone (1967).

18. Gamson's definition of structural conduciveness in terms of the extent to which communities possess distinct solidary groups is problematic in that conflict tends to raise group visibility. Thus, the effect could work both ways, with conflict increasing conduciveness as well as vice versa. However, as will be seen, the findings of the present study are inconsistent with *both* possibilities, that is, three out of four of the districts ranking highest on overall conflict ranked low on our measure of conduciveness.

19. As noted earlier, the central findings of this study do not rely upon the precise order of our rankings. However, those interested may find the complete case study data in Boyd (1973).

20. However, it is noteworthy that Gamson himself used only a few and very similar structural indicators in his research and also had limited success in differentiating high and low conflict communities according to his theoretical framework. He found that the extent to which towns were experiencing shifts in political control—his indicator of structural strain—differentiated nine "rancorous" conflict towns from nine "conventional" conflict towns with some exceptions. His measures of structural integration helped explain some of the exceptions while two measures of conduciveness failed to differentiate the two kinds of communities.

21. It should be noted that our approach is not strictly comparable with that of Gamson since we were concerned with accounting for *overall* conflict while he focused on *rancorous* conflict, namely that "characterized by the belief that norms about the waging of political conflict in American communities have been violated" (1966: 71). However, the rancorous dimension, as defined by Gamson, was included in our determination of the ranking of the districts on the *intensity* of conflict; this ranking, which is highly correlated with the conflict *incidence* ranking, is as a result quite similar to the *overall* conflict ranking. Thus, the essential categorization of the districts, that is, as to high or low on conflict, remains constant.

22. Of course, in more heterogeneous communities (suburban or otherwise) than the ones we studied, both the public and private-regarding cultures may be strongly represented and the tension which is likely to exist between these cultures may tend to produce a more complex style of political behavior than that we describe in our findings.

23. Significantly, in a review of the literature on social and political participation in urban areas, Marshall (1968: 216) found that two of the greatest faults in existing research—which mainly concentrates on *who* participates and *how much* they participate—are (1) a lack of attention to the *quality* (or type) or participation, and (2) a lack of attention to the "effect of *different* types of participation on individuals and the political system."

24. Indeed, a recent study of school-community conflict (Weeres, 1971) analyzes the factors involved in some situations where the organizational skills of higher status populaces were used to mobilize conflict.

25. Since the extent to which efficiency and expertise are prized is, of course, a matter which appears to be heavily influenced by the level of management resources as well as by the cultural ethos, rather than treating this dimension separately we will deal with it now and again, when relevant, in the course of the remainder of this paper.

26. Significantly, in his study of 15 Chicago suburban elementary school districts, O'Shea (1971) had similar findings. In five of the eight blue-collar districts he studied, there were persons serving on the school boards who were also active as leaders in local political organizations. This was not true in any of the seven white-

collar districts he studied. O'Shea also found, as did the present study, that political parties were the most important local organizations in blue-collar districts, while civic organizations were most important in white-collar districts.

27. We do not mean to imply in any of our discussion of the middle class and their public-regarding culture that white-collar populaces are fundamentally altruistic, morally upright, and so forth. Rather, we are simply calling attention to the effects of their general obedience to a certain set of norms and values governing their public behavior. For a penetrating analysis of the enlightened self-interest of public-regarding populaces, see Peterson (forthcoming, 1976).

28. Note, however, that because our deviant cases are indeed atypical—in relation to Minar's finding that lower status districts tend to have higher levels of conflict than do higher status districts, a finding which our data suggest is generalizable to Chicago suburbia as a whole—they do not contradict the overall pattern of our theoretical analysis.

29. We do not pretend to have employed scientific measures of the notoriously vague "leadership" concept. Instead, the conclusions presented here are based on *gross* differences in leadership behavior with respect to external school affairs which became apparent in the comparative analysis of the districts.

30. For the complete analysis of the deviant cases, see Boyd (1973).

31. Regarding the possibility that a "power elite" might have orchestrated this controversy to protect its interest, all respondents agreed that power in the community was essentially amorphous and that community influentials were about equally divided on the first two referenda.

32. It also should be noted that the superintendent—a key participant who might have tried to steer the board toward more realistic decisions—observed when interviewed that he could not understand the unwillingness of citizens to do what was "best" educationally. He elaborated on this theme by stating, in effect, that he took what amounted to an altruistic view of citizens' responsibilities and of politics in general because he had been raised in the La Follette "progressive" tradition.

33. By contrast, in Alton and Weston (the two low status/high conflict districts) there was lively competition between local political parties.

34. A number of analyses, for example, of city political "machines" and one-party states in the South, conclude that dominant political parties tend to reduce or depress the level of public conflict concerning governmental policy. For an example of a study of educational politics which makes this point, see Weeres (1971).

35. The census data on our districts—which do not indicate significantly greater heterogeneity in the blue-collar than in the white-collar districts—along with our findings that three out of four of the blue-collar districts were high on structural conduciveness (and all four were low on structural integration) and three out of four of the white-collar districts were low on conduciveness (and three out of four were high on integration) are consistent with this interpretation.

36. The significance of patterns of political culture, of course, extends beyond cities and suburbs to states and regions of the United States and, indeed, helps to account for important differences in political behavior among the nations of the world. See Pye (1968); Elazar (1970); and Almond and Verba (1963).

37. For a critique of the "theory," see Wolfinger and Field (1966); for a rebuttal of Wolfinger and Field's argument, see Lineberry and Fowler (1967).

38. Although we can see little substantive advantage to be gained by the semantics involved, researchers may wish to consider avoiding the invidious distinctions evoked for some by the public (altruistic ?) and private (selfish ?) regarding concep-

tualization—an objective which might be accomplished by employing Wilson and Banfield's (1971) revised conceptualization (in which the public-regarding ethos becomes the "unitary ethos," and the private-regarding ethos, the "individualist ethos") or, possibly, by utilizing Gans' (1962) closely analogous "object-orientation/person-orientation" conceptualization.

39. This point is made very clearly by Greer and Orleans (1962: 634) in their discussion of what they call the "parapolitical" structure, which consists of "ostensibly nonpolitical organizations which can represent, in political terms if necessary, an area of autonomous social value."

40. At the same time, of course, the ideology of school administrators that they are nonpolitical educational experts working in the best interests of all children has provided and, to some extent, continues to provide them with some strategic political advantages in dealing with public. However, in the face of the increasing politicization of education, this traditional ideology seems to be giving way to one which is more realistic in a number of respects. On the strategic advantages of the "old" ideology, see Wirt and Kirst (1972: 8-9).

41. On the realities of the alleged dichotomy between administration and policy-making, see Walden (1967).

42. As Peterson (1972: 3-4) has noted:

The values of schools often run contrary to the values of lower middle and working class neighborhoods within America's central cities. The enlightened educational elite seek progressive curriculum changes in mathematics, sciences, and social studies; the introduction of sex education in schools, the elimination of patronage from the recruitment process (for even clerical and custodial tasks); and even higher salaries and even more administrative positions for those staffing the system. Moreover school professionals have generally opposed aid to parochial schools. All of these policies run contrary to the values and interests of the working, often Catholic, homeowner and taxpayer.

43. The idea of fitting the system to the people to be served by it may seem novel, but we hope it will not be dimissed out of hand. Indeed, some rather strong arguments in favor of partisan school government have been advanced in recent years, especially by Iannaccone (1967) and by Salisbury (1967). However, our findings suggest that an attempt to impose partisanship on upper status, public-regarding communities may be as misguided as the attempt to nurture nonpartisanship in lower status, private-regarding communities.

REFERENCES

ALMOND, G. and S. VERBA (1963) The Civic Culture. Princeton: Princeton Univ. Press.

BACHRACH, P. and M. S. BARATZ (1962) "Two faces of power." Amer. Polit. Sci. Rev. 56, 4 (December): 947-952.

BANFIELD, E. C. and J. Q. WILSON (1963) City Politics. New York: Vintage.

BOYD, W. L. (1973) "Community status, citizen participation, and conflict in suburban school politics." Ph.D. dissertation, University of Chicago.

CAMPBELL, A. K. (1968) "Who governs the schools?" Saturday Rev. (December 21): 50ff.

COLEMAN, J. S. (1957) Community Conflict. Glencoe: Free Press.

CONNOLLY, W. E. (1974) The Terms of Political Discourse. Lexington, Mass.: Heath.

COSER, L. A. (1956) The Functions of Social Conflict. New York: Free Press.

CRAIN, R. L. (1969) The Politics of School Desegregation. New York: Anchor.

——— and D. B. ROSENTHAL (1967) "Community status as a dimension of local decision-making." Amer. Socio. Rev. 32, 6 (December): 970-984.

CRENSON, M. (1971) The Unpolitics of Air Pollution: A Study of Non-decision-making in the Cities. Baltimore: Johns Hopkins Press.

EASTON, D. (1965) A Systems Analysis of Political Life. New York: Wiley.

ELAZAR, D. (1970) Cities of the Prairie. New York: Basic Books.

ELIOT, T. E. (1959) "Toward an understanding of public school politics." Amer. Polit. Sci. Rev. 53, 4 (December): 1032-1051.

GANS, H. (1962) The Urban Villagers. New York: Free Press.

GAMSON, W. A. (1966) "Rancorous conflict in community politics." Amer. Socio. Rev. 31, 1 (February): 71-81.

GREER, S. and P. ORLEANS (1962) "The mass society and the parapolitical structure." Amer. Socio. Rev. 27, 5 (October): 634-646.

GUSFIELD, J. R. (1962) "Mass society and extremist politics." Amer. Socio. Rev. 27, 1 (February): 19-30.

HAWLEY, W. D. and F. M. WIRT [eds.] (1968) The Search for Community Power. Englewood Cliffs: Prentice-Hall.

HORTON, J. E. and W. E. THOMPSON (1962) "Powerlessness and political negativism: a study in defeated referendums." Amer. J. of Sociology 67, 5 (March): 485-493.

IANNACCONE, L. (1967) Politics in Education. New York: Center for Applied Research in Education.

JAMES, H. T., THOMAS, J. A., and H. J. DYCK (1963) Wealth, Expenditures and Decision Making for Education. School of Education, Stanford University.

KIRKENDALL, R. S. (1966) "Discriminating social, economic and political characteristics of changing versus stable policy making systems in school districts." Ph.D. dissertation. Claremont Graduate School.

KIRST, M. W. [ed.] (1970) The Politics of Education at the Local, State and Federal Levels. Berkeley: McCutchan.

——— and E. K. MOSHER (1969) "Politics of education." Rev. of Educational Research 39, 5 (December): 623-639.

KORNHAUSER, W. (1959) The Politics of Mass Society. Glencoe: Free Press.

LEVIN, M. B. (1960) The Alienated Voter. New York: Holt, Rinehart & Winston.

LINEBERRY, R. L. and E. P. FOWLER (1967) "Reformism and public policies in American cities." Amer. Polit. Sci. Rev. 61, 3 (September): 701-716.

LIPSET, S. M. (1960) Political Man. Garden City, New York: Doubleday.

LYKE, R. F. (1968) "Suburban school politics." Ph.D. dissertation. New Haven: Yale University.

MARCH, J. G. (1966) "The power of power," pp. 30-70 in D. Easton [ed.] Varieties of Political Theory. Englewood Cliffs: Prentice-Hall.

MARSHALL, D. R. (1968) "Who participates in what? A bibliographic essay on individual participation in urban areas." Urban Affairs Q. 4, 2 (December): 201-223.

MERANTO, P. J. (1970) School Politics in the Metropolis. Columbus, Ohio: Merrill.

MERELMAN, R. M. (1968) "On the neo-elitist critique of community power." Amer. Polit. Sci. Rev. 62 (June): 451-460.

MINAR, D. W. (1967) "Community politics and school board." Amer. School Board J. 154, 3 (March): 33-38.

——— (1966a) "The community basis of conflict in school system politics." Amer. Socio. Review 31, 6 (December): 822-834.

——— (1966b) Educational Decision-Making in Suburban Communities. Cooperative Research Project No. 2440. Evanston: Northwestern University.

O'SHEA, D. (1971) "School board-community relations and local resource utilization." Ph.D. dissertation, University of Chicago.

PETERSON, P. E. (forthcoming 1976) Chicago School Politics: Bargaining and Unitary Models of Policy-Formation. Chicago: Univ. of Chicago Press.

——— (1974) "The politics of American education," in F. N. Kerlinger and J. B. Carroll [eds.] Review of Research in Education, 2. Itasca, Ill.: Peacock.

——— (1972) "The school busing controversy: redistributive or pluralist politics?" Administrator's Notebook 20, 9 (May).

PYE, L. W. (1968) "Political culture," pp. 218-225 in D. L. Sills [ed.] Internatl. Encyclopedia of Social Science 12. New York: Macmillan and Free Press.

SALISBURY, R. H. (1967) "Schools and politics in the big city." Harvard Educational Rev. 37, 3 (Summer): 408-424.

SCOTT, W. R. (1970) Social Processes and Social Structures. New York: Holt, Rinehart & Winston.

SNOW, R. J. (1967) "Community resources and conflict propensity as sources for constraints on the local school administrator." Paper presented at Amer. Educational Research Assn. Annual Meeting (February). New York.

——— (1966) "Local experts: their roles as conflict managers in municipal and educational government." Ph.D. dissertation. Evanston: Northwestern University.

VIDICH, A. J. and J. BENSMAN (1958) Small Town in Mass Society. Princeton: Princeton Univ. Press.

WALDEN, J. C. (1967) "School board changes and superintendent turnover." Administrator's Notebook 15, 5 (January).

WEERES, J. B. (1971) "School-community conflict in a large urban school system." Administrator's Notebook 19, 9 (May).

WILSON, J. Q. and E. C. BANFIELD (1971) "Political ethos revisited." Amer. Polit. Sci. Rev. 65, 4 (December): 1048-1062.

WIRT, F. M. (1970) "Theory and research needs in the study of American educational politics." J. of Educational Administration 8, 1 (May): 53-87.

——— and M. W. KIRST (1972) The Political Web of American Schools. Boston: Little, Brown.

WOLFINGER, R. E. (1971) "Nondecisions and the study of local politics." Amer. Polit. Sci. Rev. 65 (December): 1063-1080.

——— and J. O. FIELD (1966) "Political ethos and the structure of city government." Amer. Polit. Sci. Rev. 60, 2 (June): 306-326.

WOOD, R. C. (1959) Suburbia: Its People and Their Politics. Boston: Houghton Mifflin.